The Xenophobe's Guide to The Dutch

Rodney Bolt

ЯR

RAVETTE BOOKS

Published by Ravette Publishing Ltd.
P.O. Box 296
Horsham
West Sussex RH13 8FH
Telephone: (01403) 711443

Editor – Catriona Tulloch Scott
Series Editor – Anne Tauté

Cover design – Jim Wire
Printer – Cox & Wyman Ltd.
Production – Oval Projects Ltd.

An **Oval Project**
produced for
Ravette Publishing.

Contents

The Dutch population is 15 million (compared with 5 million Danes; 10 million Belgians; 48 million English; 57 million French, and 80 million Germans).

The Netherlands is half the size of Scotland, not quite as large as Denmark, and could fit into Spain 12 times.

Nationalism and Identity

Forewarned

The Dutch character is inextricably bound up with the Dutch landscape. Holland is so flat that even the black and white cows stand silhouetted against the skyline. Consequently the Dutch are used to distant horizons and lots of light. Openness, freedom and vision are fundamental. Few Dutch people could be happy living in a forest. When one of The Netherlands' most famous novelists sent his parents on their first trip to Switzerland, as a present for their 50th wedding anniversary, he was surprised that they returned after only a day or two. His mother had been bitterly disappointed. She had no view from her hotel window, she explained, there were mountains in the way.

The Dutch landscape is mild and uneventful. Intrusions, such as trees, occur in orderly lines and patterns. Water, which threatens to overrun the whole country, is neatly channelled into straight canals. Control and moderation are important in behaviour too. "High trees catch a lot of wind," the Dutch warn. They describe excess in terms of *overvloed*, a 'flooding over' – as if the waters had burst the dykes. In Holland, extravagant people don't waste money, they 'spill' it.

Holland is light, but not bright – a world of greens, greys and browns. This colour scheme is repeated in the cities, where buildings are mainly of brown brick, and local bye-laws often state that residents must paint their front doors in the same shade of green. When Van Gogh forsook his native country for the brighter, bumpier regions of the south of France, he left off painting in the cosy, gravy browns of The Potato Eaters, took to gaudier hues and went mad.

How They See Themselves

From the comfort of their immaculate sitting rooms the Dutch may acknowledge that they are the cleanest people on earth, are thrifty, have a canny head for business, an unparalleled facility with languages, an unequalled ability to get along with one another and with foreigners, and an inimitable charm. But they will be far too modest, unless pushed, to admit publicly that all this makes them somewhat superior to other nations.

Above all the Dutch pride themselves on their tolerance and flexibility; qualities which, in addition to carrying moral kudos, are good for business. The blanket of benevolence is not a woolly liberal one, but is woven from the sound stuff of commerce. It is quite thick enough to cover niggling inconsistencies, such as a secret mistrust of Moroccans, distaste at foreign cooking smells from the apartment downstairs, or scores of white people blacking up as caricatured negro slaves on St. Nicholas's Day. Picking out such contradictions is the surest way to hurt a Dutch person's feelings.

How Others See Them

Most nations regard the Dutch as organized and efficient – rather like the Germans, but not as awesome. One can hardly be frightened, the reasoning goes, of a nation of rosy-cheeked farmers who live in windmills and have clogs at the bottom of the wardrobe, tulips in the garden and piles of round cheese in the larder.

But the Dutch also have a reputation for being opinionated, stubborn, and incorrigibly mean. The Belgians go even further, and complain that their neighbours are downright devious in business affairs. Generally, though, other nations see them as forthright to a fault. Dutch frankness completely overwhelms more reticent peoples, such as the Japanese who find the Dutch the rudest and most arrogant of the Europeans they do business with – though they are impressed by Dutch acumen as traders. "Where a Dutchman has passed, not even the grass grows any more," say the Japanese.

The English survey the Dutch with guarded approval, as the closest any Continentals come to the sacrosanct state of being English. Such chumminess has not always prevailed. In the 17th century these two seafaring nations were at each other's throats. An English pamphlet raged: "A Dutchman is a Lusty, Fat, Two-legged Cheeseworm. A Creature that is so addicted to eating Butter, Drinking Fat and Sliding [skating] that all the world knows him for a slippery fellow". The English language gained a whole new list of pejoratives, including 'Dutch courage' (booze-induced bravery), 'Dutch comfort' ('things could be worse') and 'Dutch gold' (fake). Nowadays there is an echo of this attitude in the tendency of some English people (especially customs officers) to see the Dutch as a nation of drug-dazed pornographers. But on the whole the Dutch score top marks for cabling BBC television to every home in the land and speaking English without flinching or causing a flinch.

How They Would Like Others to See Them

The Dutch would like to be held up as The Ultimate Europeans. To this end they have assiduously assimilated so much from the nations around them that they have almost done away with their own cultural identity. This is a good thing, as it is the logical result of Dutch flexibility and tolerance. It also means that most people find something familiar about the Dutch. This guarantees that everyone likes them.

That Holland is the small boy in the class of Europe doesn't unduly bother either its residents or its politicians. By making enough noise and having an opinion about everything even a small boy can be noticed. With luck he might even become class captain – a job that, with his insider's knowledge of unfairness and oppression, he knows he can do more justly than some other class members he might care to mention. Especially those with a history of bullying.

How They See Others

Despite the fact that they have for centuries been edging their country toward the British Isles, the Dutch feel ambivalent about the English. They are surprised that these rather puny islanders, who clam up when one talks to them about sex, somehow manage to write such good books and – in their amateurish way – to run some of the world's best banks (which the Dutch are all too willing to snap up at bargain prices when they collapse). The Dutch think that the English are cottagey and a bit twee, but they adore English underwear and are dumbfounded that such an uptight nation could produce such elegant and practical designs. One Dutch television interviewer couldn't resist asking Margaret Thatcher whether she bought her underwear at Marks & Spencer. "Doesn't everyone?" was the stately reply.

France and Italy may be suitable places to holiday, but the Dutch view their inhabitants with a twinge of disapproval. The French are too frivolous to win the lasting admiration of a nation that has Calvin in its bones, and besides, say the Dutch, they are obstructionists with no sense of tolerance or skill at negotiation. A nation that allows its farmers to pile turnips on the motorway must be viewed with some scepticism.

Forthrightness may be a virtue, but extravagantly flaunting your emotions smacks of lack of control – and so the Italians (and most other Mediterraneans) join the ranks of the 'tolerated-but-not-quite-as-good-as-us'. Of all the European nations, the Dutch admire the Swiss. Their country is spotless, their banks unassailable and their personal bank accounts are secret.

Special Relationships

Tolerance has its limits. The first barrier that Dutch tolerance comes up against is the German border. There is no one more likely to rouse the Dutch from their customary cheerfully benign state than a German. The Dutch see the Germans as arrogant, noisy, rigid and intolerant – everything in fact that the Dutch are not. They are wary of a nation that shows such a passion for living in forests. But usually they don't even bother to try and explain. They simply do not like Germans. Telling a Dutch person that their language seems very similar to German is unlikely to benefit your relationship. Remarking that the two nations seem rather alike in many ways will probably get you thrown out of the house.

If a German asks for directions in a Dutch city, a Dutch person will point to the border or the nearest international railway station. When the Dutch spot a German in the street, they will shout "Where's my bike?" and burst into gales of laughter. This is an in joke referring to the fact that the Germans confiscated all bicycles during the Second World War. Dutch people of all ages make this joke. They will do it even if their *parents* are not old enough to have experienced the Occupation. Anything to knock the Germans down a notch or two.

Holland's southern border also presents a bit of a stumbling block. Apart from the Afrikaners in South Africa and the inhabitants of a few scattered ex-colonies, the Belgians are the only people in the world who speak a language anything like Dutch. One might think that this would endear their southern cousins to the Hollanders, but the Dutch regard the Belgians as laughably dim, and fit only for derision:

Q: "What is written on the bottom of a Belgian milk bottle?"
A: "Open other end."

Often these jokes take on a somewhat surreal quality:

Q: "What is written on the bottom of a Belgian swimming pool?"
A: "No Smoking."

Q: "Why are Belgian glasses square?"
A: "So they don't leave a round mark on the table."

In The Netherlands itself, the inhabitants of the most southerly province of Limburg (whose capital is the infamous Maastrict) are saddled with the reputation of being stupid, hence:

Q: "What happens when a person from Maastricht goes to live in Belgium?"
A: "The average IQ of both nations rises."

Character

Open Minds

The Dutch tolerate prostitutes displaying themselves in windows on street-corners, men cuddling each other in public, coffeeshops that sell marijuana over the counter, and the quirky habits of immigrants and refugees from all over the world. They distribute free needles to heroin addicts, allow prisoners conjugal rights and give teenagers abortion on request. They even tolerate people's insistence on calling their country 'Holland', when Holland is in fact a province of The Netherlands.

Tolerance is not simply a virtue, it is a national duty. With 370 people for every square kilometre, Holland is Europe's most densely populated country. If the Dutch didn't forgive – or at least ignore – each other's foibles and peculiar inclinations, life itself would become intolerable. Tolerance is really pragmatism in disguise, and so counts as a good, solid Protestant value.

Even if they see something that, secretly, they find rather shocking, the Dutch will appear unruffled – provided that it does not infringe on their own freedom. A deep respect for people's freedom to live their own lives, in their own way, is as Dutch as dykes and windmills. The Dutch place the bounds to behaviour along lines that reflect a tacit understanding of just how far you can go before knocking down the invisible walls of privacy and personal liberty. Life behind these walls is at the same time public, yet nobody else's business.

Judging where the boundaries lie is never easy. On Remembrance Day the two-minute silence is generally and movingly observed. Trams, cars and people come to a halt. An immigrant family unaware of the reverence of the occasion continued on their way, talking noisily amongst

11

a sea of solemn faces. The Dutch were caught: to scold foreign refugees would seem intolerant; they had broken the unwritten rules, but then how were they to know? Should they be told? And so the reasoning tumbles on, ruining the moment in somersaults of moral confusion.

Open Curtains

The Dutch are open about everything. Preserved vegetables come in glass jars rather than in tins. Lavatories have a shelf in the bowl, ensuring that even your internal workings are open to daily inspection.

To assure their neighbours, and themselves, that they have nothing to hide, the Dutch build houses with big windows and do not draw their curtains at night. You can watch your neighbours' television, see what they are having for dinner, note whether they shout at their children and fervently exercise your powers of tolerance if you notice anything untoward.

Clean windows are the primary concern of any householder, and rooms are lit with a subtle chiaroscuro that presents a cosy picture to the street at night. Rather than draw the blinds, people whose houses open directly on to the street hang little screens made out of wooden-framed doilies in the windows, or stick narrow strips of clouded plastic to the glass. These are positioned to avoid tiresome eye-contact with passers-by, while still leaving the room open to public view. But no Dutch person would dream of staring in at the windows. That would be an invasion of privacy. The openness is there to reassure them that they are living in a free and friendly community.

Openness is also important in personal relationships. This leads to perfect frankness, which other nations may find disarming. If you are suffering from a particularly unfortunate haircut, an English friend might tactfully suggest that you wear that nice hat you bought last week. A Dutch person will ask you what on earth has happened to your hair.

Gezelligheid

Gezelligheid is the Dutch nirvana. Dictionaries ineptly translate *gezelligheid* as 'cosiness'. The German *Gemütlichkeit* comes a little nearer the mark, but that nation has order rather than conviviality as its ultimate goal. A Dutch historian has described *gezelligheid* as "partly a sort of cosiness and partly a living togetherness". The mood in a neighbourhood café on a cold winter's afternoon is *gezellig*; a mother will call "Keep it *gezellig*!" if she hears her offspring becoming dangerously boisterous; a popular Dutch beer is advertised as 'guaranteed *gezellig*'. Rather than switch on the lights at twilight, a family will light a few candles, make a pot of coffee and sit looking out of their large clean window, suffusing themselves in *gezelligheid*.

Living on top of each other as they do, the Dutch have discovered that the best way to get on is by making sure that everything is always *gezellig*. Life runs according to a subtle decorum. The Dutch don't say "What will the neighbours think?", but "Think of the neighbours!"

If you drive in the wrong direction up a quiet one way street at two o'clock in the morning and meet the police head-on, they will probably pull over and let you pass. There are more important things to do than arresting someone who is doing so little harm. Besides, it would not be *gezellig*. Dutch tolerance is the moral face of *gezelligheid*.

Going Dutch

This is the nation that has come up with a scraper for getting the last remnants of the film of milk from the inside of a milk bottle. The Dutch 'think with their pockets'. Parsimony is not an embarrassment, but a virtue. On trains you will see people encouraging their dogs to sit in their holdalls. This is because the dog then qualifies as 'hand baggage' rather than 'accompanying pet', and so is not eligible for a ticket. Rather than objecting, ticket inspectors regard this as admirable ingenuity.

Expenditure is acceptable only when there is hope of realising a profit (*de kost gaat voor de baat uit* – the cost comes before the benefit). Otherwise it's a case of *elk dubbeltje omdraaien* – turning over each coin twice before even thinking of spending it. 'Going Dutch' was invented so that the Dutch could sit back and enjoy their coffee in peace, without worrying about who was going to pick up the bill.

Yes, But...

For the Dutch, the other side of the question is as important as the question itself. Dialogue is the lubricant of tolerance, and the essential ingredient of dialogue is "Yes, but...". In Holland the campaign against smoking in offices had the slogan 'We can talk about it'. The pro-smoking lobby was an acknowledged force long before, in other countries, it had even begun to be a backlash.

Nowadays squatters enter into dialogue with landlords and the city council, and drug dealers sit down to cosy chats with the police. Opposition is by negotiation rather than confrontation. Whereas Americans make do with two political parties, the Dutch have around a dozen – but they have a coalition government. This is more *gezellig*.

Having an Opinion

Discourse on death or sexual deviance may cause other nations to squirm, euphemize or change the topic, but will have the Dutch frankly and happily airing an opinion. When they find themselves somewhat shocked by a theme, then tolerance will start firing on all cylinders and the conversation will hurtle on. If, after a while, nobody has voluntarily come up with an alternative opinion, the conversation will momentarily pause, someone will politely offer a "Yes, but..." or an "On the other hand...", and travel will resume in a new direction. Tolerance requires that issues be examined from all sides.

The only topics that are exceptions to this rule are income and the Queen. Minor members of the royal family may be exposed to the occasional guarded or sceptical remark, but criticising or joking about "Our Queen" will bring conversation to an awkward halt. Discussing what you earn and how much you spend on rent, your clothes or your car will elicit far deeper disapproval from a Dutch person than admitting what you might get up to in bed. The only time that personal finances are considered in any way suitable material for conversation is after a visit to the dentist. Then everyone can join in talk about bridges and crowns and the horrific row of figures at the foot of dentists' bills.

Apart from the state of one's teeth, other Dutch conversational warmers include football and the weather. The patterns are the same in either case: a brief comment on the present state of play, a remark or two about the previous week's offerings and speculation about things to come. Then you can move on to general analysis and the stating of opinions.

Beliefs and Values

Merchant Values

The Dutch are traders at heart, and have a few centuries of outstanding success in the field to back up their belief that business rules. *Handel is handel* – 'trade is trade' – is considered a justifiable excuse for any apparent hypocrisy, be it selling mercury that poisons the workers in South American goldmines, or extending airport runways while at the same time deploring the effect of jets on the environment. When a 17th-century munitions dealer was accused of supplying the enemy he retorted "If we didn't sell to them, we couldn't afford to fight them". This logic was considered acceptable then, and it still is today, when questions are raised about selling equipment to Iraq.

Somewhere in the shadows behind every diligent trader lurks the Protestant work ethic. The Dutch believe that they were all born miserable sinners, and that this world is a place to work and suffer in.

They have even had to make their own land to live on, reclaiming it from the sea. "God created the earth, but the Dutch made The Netherlands", the saying goes. Later, because they are so tolerant, they will get to heaven – but that is unlikely to affect God's attitude one jot, and they will probably have to toil and sweat up there too. In the meantime, *Arbeid adelt* ('work makes noble'), and 'laziness is the devil's pillow'.

The Wagging Finger

The spirit of tolerance does constant battle with the ghost of Calvin for control of the Dutch psyche. Few Dutch people go to church any more, but they don't need to. Inside every Hollander's head is a little pulpit containing a preacher with a *vermanende vinger*, a wagging finger. Laziness and immoderation are the main themes of his sermon. His business is to provide a nagging Protestant conscience. Often he is let loose to admonish the outside world.

Dirty windows, behaviour that is not *gezellig* (lager louts and German tourists are the main culprits here) and flashy extravagance will all set a Dutch person's own finger wagging. But most of all the *vermanende vinger* is there to ensure respectability. The impulse towards becoming a good, solid citizen is irresistible. Even cannabis traders have formed an association that exercises quality control and ensures that members pay their taxes.

The only thing that can severely inhibit the *vermanende vinger* is a powerful counter-impulse from the duty to be tolerant or the suggestion of financial profit.

Calvin Rules

Protestant values are so firmly planted in Dutch soil that it comes as a surprise to most people to find that 35% of the population are registered as Roman Catholic. Traditionally, the Catholics occupy a patch in the south-east, while the rest of the country (including all the big cities) is mainly Protestant. But for centuries Calvinism has ruled with such a firm hand that even the Church of Rome has responded to its grip. Catholics, too, show a good Protestant penchant for hard work and sober living.

In days of yore, Catholics were tolerated (of course), but had to worship inconspicuously, behind closed doors, in churches built to look like houses. Today, despite their separate schools and television station, it still seems as if Holland's Catholics are living behind a solidly built Protestant façade – though they do manage to send shudders down nearly every spine in the Vatican by forming splinter groups that demand tolerance of divorce and contraception, and wives for priests.

The Sabbath is the one day that the Dutch can stop working without too much of a conscience. Most dedicate their Sundays to tennis, watching football and walking the dog; but in rural areas whole villages turn out en masse for church, walking hooked together two-by-two, wearing hats and their sober Sunday best and rolling off withering looks to anyone so frivolous as to ride a bicycle or mow the lawn.

Pillars of the Community

The pillars of the Dutch Establishment are not individuals, but institutions. For centuries Dutch society has rested firmly on the two pillars (*zuilen*) of the Protestant and Catholic churches. More recently, trendy socialist and ethnic columns have been added to the colonnade. There are still separate Protestant and Catholic universities, trades unions, television channels and political parties.

People may nowadays treat them interchangeably, but to chip away at this segregation would be to invite dreadful collapse. In rural areas especially, the borders are still fiercely defended. A small village with a Protestant, a Catholic and a Montessori school may not have enough pupils to go round, but each establishment would sooner close down than merge with any of the others.

Oddly, this perception that society is made up of different *zuilen* goes hand-in-hand with the Dutch belief in tolerance: mutually exclusive world views need not be mutually destructive, but can jointly prop up a sturdy *gezellige* whole.

Zuilen are also very comforting. Building yourself into a *zuil* means that you don't have to get involved with the nitty-gritty of actually integrating with anything you consider foreign, but can still congratulate yourself on accepting it as a separate though essential part of society. It was the descendants of Dutch settlers in South Africa who, perverting this reasoning, invented *Apartheid*.

Wealth and Success

The pursuit of wealth is a favourite Dutch pastime, and accumulating money is a virtue. Spending it is a vice. A healthy bank balance may be proof that you are shouldering your earthly burden of hard work, but it is a private assurance.

The Dutch consider a flashy display of worldly goods as extreme bad taste. Discussing your salary is anathema. When one national magazine published a list of Holland's top ten richest people, they had to follow it the next week with an apology to one of the millionaires for placing him too high up on the list – though he begrudgingly admitted that he might be the fourteenth richest man in the country.

This is not to say that the Dutch deny themselves material comfort. It is perfectly acceptable to surround yourself with *degelijke spullen* – good, sound objects that work efficiently. They may even be stylish, but never ostentatious. A modest Mercedes might pass muster; a Rolls Royce would raise a disapproving eyebrow. Even the grandest Dutch homes present a narrow, low-key façade to the street, but, in private behind it, stretch out into spacious rooms and secluded gardens.

Class

The Dutch pride themselves on their egalitarian, classless society. There may be a Queen, but she is a stolid upholder of *burgelijke* (respectable middle-class) values rather than a fairytale monarch. Dutch citizens don't have to bow or curtsey to her, and she was 'invested' rather than crowned.

A tiny handful of old families, together with a selection of graduates from long-established universities, make up a small, self-supporting Old Boys' network that is spun through big business, banking and the diplomatic corps. The rest of Holland belongs to a sprawling middle-class that laughs at snobbery and gets along quite happily with itself. At one end of the spectrum are the university-educated professionals who watch the BBC on cable; at the other are the workers who soak up soaps and sensationalist magazines. But, unlike the English, they speak a mutually comprehensible language and play life by similar rules.

Behaviour

The Family

A glance at the entries in the Births column of a Dutch newspaper reveals the Dutch veneration for their children: 'Born to Piet and Maria, a new world citizen, Hans, 4/6/95'.

The Dutch family is the kernel of *gezelligheid* and an academy for learning the skills of negotiation and tolerance. The Dutch treat children with respect, and expect them swiftly to pick up the trappings of respectability. From an early age children learn to "Keep it *gezellig*" and conduct themselves in a way that doesn't ruffle the feathers of those that surround them. "*Doe maar gewoon, dan doe je al gek genoeg*" ("Behave normally, that's mad enough") they are often told – and in Holland this is usually true.

The young are credited with the intelligence to make decisions about their lives. When planning changes to a local playground, a Dutch borough council will send questionnaires to children rather than to parents. Even situations where 'Mummy knows best' are open to negotiation. Complicated deals are struck in supermarket aisles as dinner options are discussed, spinach and broccoli being traded off against strawberry ice-cream and extra cookies.

Unlike the English, who uphold the structures and strictures of Victorian family values, the Dutch allow families to take on some adventurous shapes, and do so with warmth and verve. Granny and grandpa, sitting down to Christmas lunch with their eldest son, his boyfriend, their unmarried daughter and her children, make a cosier gathering than many an English family unit complete with one parent of each sex and 2.5 noisome brats.

Animals

An old Dutch commonplace holds that 'If a Hollander should be bereft of his pipe of tobacco, he could not blissfully enter heaven'. Nowadays, for 'pipe of tobacco' read 'dog'. In such a populous country, you would expect more compact pets – such as budgies, hamsters or goldfish – to be the norm, but it is the bounding, jolly, slobber-over-everything-and-defecate-everywhere mutt that is the Dutch person's best friend. There is no escape. Dogs have free range over parks, shops, cafés and restaurants.

The national obsession with cleanliness suffers a serious blip when it comes to dogs' dirt. Pavements are turned into obstacle courses. For pedestrians it is a case of eyes down, forget window shopping and leave your deep-tread soles at home. Paving stones painted with a picture of a squatting dog, an arrow and the words *In de Goot* (In the Gutter) are sniffed at and ignored. The people may be multi-lingual but their dogs are illiterate.

The Elderly

Alongside dogs and children, elders occupy a prime place in the Dutch pantheon – and they are determined to stay there. The younger generation may be beginning to mutter about the 'grey plague', but they are firmly put in their place. Grey power sees to that: after a lifetime of toil, the '65-plus' brigade felt they deserved a bit of fun, formed their own political party, and succeeded in winning six seats in the national parliament. Unfortunately old age was about all they could agree on. A succession of quarrels split their ranks so now they stand as independents, and seek satisfaction in representing themselves and in voicing a lifetime's opinions.

When the elderly are not campaigning for better pensions, they may be found belting their lungs out in a 'grey' version of the Eurovision Song Contest, cycling about the countryside and generally having the time of their lives.

Eccentrics

It is very difficult to become an eccentric in Holland. Dutch tolerance means that all sorts of odd behaviour is simply redefined as normal. The English believe that anything is acceptable as long as it doesn't upset the horses. In Holland the cardinal rule is that all behaviour is tolerated so long as it not un-*gezellig* or bad for business.

There is a strong sense that you should not upset the apple cart or stick your head above the parapet. It is just that the Dutch apple cart can take more rocking, and the parapet is a little higher, than most other Europeans are used to – behave normally, that's mad enough...

Immigrants

The Netherlands has long been a haven for people who have begun to find the sea a little choppy in their own part of the world. As a nation of good traders, the Dutch knew that it was in their best interest to be flexible when it came to the finer points of religious or political belief. In earlier centuries Protestants fled here from Antwerp (bringing diamond cutting skills), and Jews came from Portugal (complete with news of secret trade routes). Since the Second World War, Holland has basked in the halo of the Anne Frank effect – even though, as Queen

Beatrix herself has recently made clear, the Dutch record in those troubled times was far from squeaky clean.

Today, Surinamese, Indonesians, Turks, Moroccans and refugees from the Balkans – to name just a few – live alongside the homegrown Dutch. People from former colonies, especially those from Indonesia, are now part of the warp and weave of Dutch society, but for many of the others 'living alongside' is just what they do. The Dutch retreat into their *zuilen*, and pack the immigrants up into one of their own.

Of course, everyone determinedly displays their tolerance of refugees and foreigners, and might even remark on how they've perked up local cuisine and added a dash of colour to some parts of town – it's just that things are more *gezellig* within the neat confines of your own particular compartment. In some of the darker corners of these separate drawers there are ominous mutterings about how the foreigners take up all the apartments and jobs, and how, tolerant though the Dutch would like to be, The Netherlands is, unfortunately, just too full.

Manners and Etiquette

Dutch manners have more to do with affability than rigid form. Their aim is to create a *gezellige* ambience, where everyone can relax and enjoy each other's company. Even so, there are pitfalls that can trap the unwary. You will know that you have fallen in a hole when the atmosphere suddenly cools. You may not be left in the dark for long. Dutch people will generally tell you exactly what it is that you have done wrong – then it is your turn to feel offended by their bluntness.

24

Greetings

When meeting someone for the first time, the Dutch smile, shake hands and give their name. The handshake is a warm one, someway between the German pumping iron and British brevity. Soon they will be addressing each other by first names rather than surnames, though not with the alacrity that Americans show in these matters. In the meantime they are summing each other up.

Colleagues and acquaintances stick to handshakes, which increase in duration and warmth if they approve of one another. Across the bridge, in the realms of friendship, handshaking gives way to the Dutch kiss – one peck on each cheek and a third thrown in for good measure. The Dutch shake hands or kiss on meeting and at parting, invariably and regardless of permutations in gender.

When greeting people in Holland it is useful to have some props to hand, namely flowers and coffee. The Dutch (of both sexes) exchange flowers for the flimsiest of reasons. Posies pass between them like pecks on the cheek. The next step after greeting, if it is humanly possible in the circumstances, is to have a cup of coffee.

Fingers Off

Dutch frugality restricts guests to just one piece of cake with their coffee. Acceptance of a second slice (in the rare event of your being offered one) will result in the same silent disapproval as would listing a catalogue of your woes in response to an English person's formulaic "How are you?" Helping yourself to olives or peanuts with your pre-dinner sherry will also cause brows to furrow. The distribution of such bounty is strictly the host's domain.

Dutch people confronted with a hearty "Help yourself!" at the dinner table will end up embarrassed or hungry, or both.

Gestures and Insults

The waving about of arms is one aspect of foreign culture that the Dutch have not adopted, though a wagging forefinger in the face of extravagance, intolerance or laziness is an insuppressible homegrown reflex. In moments of extreme ire the wagging forefinger may bow to a straightened middle finger, or a tap of the forehead to question someone's sanity.

Verbally, the Dutch express their disgust by damning things on behalf of God, and they insult each other with liberal reference to genitalia and bodily functions. This abuse is sometimes hard to distinguish from affection. *Scheetje* ('little fart') or *drolletje* ('little turd') are both terms of tender endearment.

With U or Without U

As they glide along the scale from acquaintanceship into friendship, the Dutch drop *U* (the formal 'you') in favour of *je* and *jij*. They do this more readily than the Germans, and many younger Dutch people don't bother with *U* at all. But many bosses and elders still expect to be called *U*, even if the conversation is quite chummy. Most people pussyfoot around, sheltering behind complicated sentence structures, until someone innocently lets drop a *je*, bringing down the barriers.

In shops, being addressed by the assistant as *U* rather than *je* is a sad indication that you have finally turned the corner into middle age. Thanks are also best expressed with a *U*. Dutch children are told to "thank with two words" – *dank u*, rather than *bedankt* (a cop-out which is short for 'you are thanked', conveniently leaving out the pronoun). Business letters should never be without *U*, and to begin a sentence in a letter with *Ik* ('I') shows an arrogance which is considered to be beyond the pale. This fervour for self-abnegation overflows into the Dutch telephone directory, where names are printed without capital letters.

Queueing

Queueing is an import to The Netherlands that has met with limited success. In busy banks and post offices queues may be controlled electronically by flashing numbers and slips of paper. People mill around disconsolately until their number comes up. In the absence of such technology they will stand in line, but the important factor is not so much the order of people in the queue as the gap between its first occupant and the person actually conducting business at the counter.

The Dutch deeply respect privacy, especially in financial affairs, and you are expected to leave at least a metre between you and whoever is taking out money or buying stamps. There is often a line drawn on the floor beyond which you may not trespass.

In shops, queueing is a more abstract affair. On entering a shop the Dutch make a mental note of who was there before them. Shop assistants abnegate all responsibility, simply calling out "Who's next?", leaving it to the customers to assert their rights of precedence, which they do in no uncertain terms. When it comes to buses, trams and trains, then elbows, umbrellas, and sheer bulk rule.

Leisure and Pleasure

Taking a break from their burden of hard work, the Dutch relax over a cup of coffee. On special occasions they may do this in each others' houses (arriving with the statutory bunch of flowers, and consuming the regulation single piece of cake), but mostly they meet in cafés. The local café is a sort of communal sitting room – cosy, smoky, and packed with people who have left their own sitting rooms empty and pristine, with the curtains open for all to see.

The primary requirement for entry into café society is an opinion. Armed with at least one opinion, a Dutch person can while away a whole evening, relatively cheaply, locked in endless verbal battle over a cup of coffee, or – as the evening progresses – a slim glass of beer. Only an important football match, bursting into life on the television in the corner, can interrupt the flow.

Holidays

The Dutch consider a break from their native climate as essential to their health and mental stability. They prefer to take their holidays somewhere soaking up the sun, and so head for the hills of France, or the sunny coasts of Greece or Spain. The success of a Dutch holiday is calculated by the resultant depth of tan and the number of days on which it did not rain. Even people on Social Security get an annual holiday allowance, so that they can go and lie in the sun somewhere and recover from the stress of being unemployed.

But this flight across the borders is where the adventure stops. In all other respects the Dutch prefer their holiday to be as *gezellig* and as Dutch as possible. The surest way of achieving this is to take your home along with you: there are nearly half a million caravans in The Netherlands. Sometimes whole neighbourhoods will set off together to create a *gezellige* corner of some foreign campsite that is forever Holland.

Caravanning has the additional advantage of being cheap. Even if they are lashing out on a holiday apartment, a Dutch family will be sure to fill the boot of their car with sacks of potatoes and other sensible Dutch provisions to protect their stomachs and pockets against the onslaughts of foreign fare, and ensure that they will not need to spend money along the way.

Sport

Most Dutch people seem satisfied with the daily exercise they get cycling, though in the winter many take to skating. When the weather gets really cold, people sharpen their skates and talk of nothing else but the *elfstedentocht*, a marathon that takes place on the canals and waterways between eleven towns in Friesland. The frisson of anticipation as to whether the freeze will be widespread enough is almost as exciting as the race itself – which is just as well, as it is hardly ever cold enough to hold the *elfstedentocht*.

Faced with Holland's flat terrain, the Dutch have come up with some sports of their own. Members of the Dutch Mountaineering Club, acting out of desperation, spend their weekends scaling the sides of tall buildings, and hundreds of other people opt for 'horizontal mountain climbing' – wading thigh deep through the black, sucking mud off the Frisian coast. This they do for hours on end, before packing up and returning home. Early in August you can witness another homegrown pastime – pole sitting. Men sit on poles in the North Sea until they fall off. The last one to do so is the winner. Endurance of discomfort rescues such sports from any un-Calvinistic tendency towards frivolity.

When it comes to watching other people braving the elements and pitting their strength against each other, the Dutch favour football above all sports. Important matches have been known to cause city councils to adjourn sessions, and supporters celebrate victories with officially sanctioned street parties. During the season, football eclipses the weather as a topic of conversation, and the remote control unit gathers dust behind the sofa as the television stays stuck on the sports channel.

Television

Holland has one of the oldest and most comprehensive cable television networks in Europe. Nearly every household in the country has at its fingertips BBC1 and BBC2, as well as German, French, Belgian and Italian national stations, and a range of local and speciality channels – a feast from which the Dutch pick and choose with relish. This suits their cultural make-up perfectly. Cable television is the modern expression of what the Dutch have been doing for centuries. They are the world's most adept cultural zappers.

The Dutch stations offer a mixed diet of foreign films, tacky game shows, overacted soaps and talk shows. Watching people ponder, argue and opine appeals to the Dutch, so talk shows notch up high ratings. The most popular ones are filmed live from cafés – an on-screen reflection of what the Dutch themselves are doing, when they are not watching television.

Sex

The Dutch preference for openness and clarity turns a bright light on to what is, for many other nations, the murky domain of sex. The English, in particular, are startled by the glare. But, as it is such a lights-on affair, sex is, for the Dutch, as much part of the clear world of reason as of the trickier realms of passion. A fully-clothed television announcer can talk freely about the necessity for safe sex against the seething backdrop of a 'Safe Sex Orgy', filmed live. The shaven-headed leader of a sado-masochists' club is interviewed (in bed), not about what its members get up to, but about how the club is organized.

When it comes to personal relationships, the Dutch are just as open. One national magazine runs a popular column in which couples pose naked (heads and surnames blotted out) and frankly discuss each other's physical attributes. The most popular television programmes are those with titles such as *Het spijt me* ('I'm sorry'), in which couples that have split up are reconciled (or not, as the case may be) in full view of the nation.

Sense of Humour

The Dutch sense of humour relishes mishap and mayhem, rather than verbal acrobatics. Someone falling through his chair on to the floor will get a bigger laugh than the bravest pun. Uncle Theo disappearing and coming back in Aunt Miep's frock goes down a great deal better than attempts at witty banter around the dinner table. Running through all this knockabout jollity is a tough, cruel streak. A good dollop of suffering and humiliation will have a Dutch audience on its knees with mirth. Despite their disdain for most things German, the Dutch revel in *Schadenfreude*.

A whiff of naughtiness and the violation of the odd taboo are also common ingredients for a good laugh. If they weren't so wary of being politically incorrect, the Dutch would adore Benny Hill. Many secretly do. Other British comedians are more openly appreciated. Given their facility with the English language and the easy accessibility of BBC Television, the Dutch are developing a taste for the UK product. British stand-up comedians – especially the ruder ones – have quite a following in Holland and are beginning to spawn Dutch imitators.

The Dutch are too frank to dabble in irony. They will take what you say at face value and interpret your carefully honed ironies as error, insult or sarcasm. But they do share with the English an ability to laugh at themselves – "How was copper wire invented?" "By two Dutchmen fighting over a *stuiver* [a copper 5c piece]". The one proviso, however, is that jibes steer clear of the Dutch royal family and the sacred territory of Dutch tolerance.

The more refined brands of Dutch humour are dry, and delight in absurdity and in turning social values topsy turvy. At times this becomes a gentle national whimsy, of the sort that results in city councils having trams covered in cartoons and bright designs, but there are strains of this humour that can leave the foreigner nonplussed: "Good God!" cries a nouveau riche, eyeing his hostess's cocktail frock and bringing party conversation to a halt: "What a fine fabric. It would make a wonderful dress!"

The most *gezellig* of all forms of humour is the good story, especially if it knocks about a little with traditional Dutch values:

On the occasion of their first-born son's first birthday, the proud parents asked him what he would like. "A pink ping-pong ball" was the answer. Respecting his decision, the father scoured Holland for a pink ping-pong ball, and finally found one. For his second birthday, the parents asked again. The two-year old asked for a basket of pink ping-pong balls. Mummy and Daddy duly obliged – though with some difficulty. For his third birthday the boy asked for a truck load of pink ping-pong balls. Still his parents respected his decision, though fulfilling the request was almost impossible. When he asked for a roomful of pink ping-pong balls for his fourth birthday, his father decided to open a pink ping-pong ball factory. He found a niche in the market, and his business met with some success. With each birthday the young lad increased his demand for pink ping-pong balls. Just before his twelfth birthday he was run down by a truck. He lay in hospital, seriously ill, but managed to respond to the question about what he wanted for his birthday in the usual way. Pink ping-pong balls had by now made his parents wealthy, and they decided it would not be an invasion of their son's privacy to ask him why he had such a passion for pink ping-pong balls. Leaning over his bed, they whispered the question in his ear. "Because...", said the boy, "Because...", and died.

Obsessions

Coffee

Coffee is a national institution. The most significant classical Dutch novel is about coffee. A cup of coffee marks all goings out and comings in. It is the point around which friendships, funerals, birthdays and office life pivot. Coffee is the essential lubricant of *gezelligheid*.

In Holland coffee is served black and strong enough to double the pulse rate. Coffee with milk is tolerated, but is considered to be almost another drink. The Dutch call it *koffie verkeerd*, literally 'coffee wrong'. Putting cream in coffee is seen as downright odd, though it is acceptable to add *koffie melk*, a kind of evaporated milk.

In cafés a cup of coffee comes complete with a small biscuit. This is as fundamental an accessory as sugar cubes or the little plastic cup of *koffie melk*. The Dutch nibble through more biscuits per annum than any other nation in Europe. The only explanation for their not being top of the coffee consumption league as well is that someone, somewhere, must be recycling used grains.

Water

Over 40% of Holland is below sea level, much of it land stolen from marshes, rivers and the ocean. The Dutch live with a constant sense of guilt about this. On one hand the situation is good for the Calvinistic psyche. The Dutch are the chosen people diligently battling against the tide, locked into a neverending and morally uplifting struggle merely to keep their heads above water. On the other hand, they live in fear of divine retribution for their cheek. The

Almighty might threaten other nations with plagues and earthquakes, but He threatens the Dutch with inundation.

When floods do occur, the stream of refugees away from the stricken areas is countered by an equal but opposite flow of sightseers who will stand and watch the waters rising with the sort of titillated awe that other nations reserve for multiple motorway pile-ups.

Bicycles

There are 13 million bicycles in The Netherlands – that's very nearly one for everybody living there. Punks, grannies, students and company directors trundle through the cities and swoop in fleets out into the countryside (especially on National Cycling Day). The Dutch parliament employs its own resident bicycle repair man, and one Dutch university even has a Professor of Bicycling.

The Dutch Bicycle is a solid, black machine which you ride in a sit-up-and-beg position. More Miss Marple than Tour de France, a 'good' Dutch bicycle will have a frame that appears to be made of cast iron, on to which are fastened working parts of an astonishing variety of vintages. The only part that can be guaranteed not to work (if it is there at all) is the front light. This does not really matter, as the first rule of the Dutch Highway Code is that the cyclist is always right, even when riding without a light, in the middle of the night in the wrong direction up a one-way street. Motorists are aware of this and take the necessary precautions.

To the Dutch mind the bicycle is more an extension of the body than a separate means of transport. People behave on bicycles as they would do if they were walking. Lovers cycle hand-in-hand. If it rains, cyclists put up their umbrellas and pedal on. They will exercise the dog by riding about, with the frisky animal tripping alongside on the end of its lead. No Dutch cyclists would ever consider that a red traffic light (or any other traffic sign for that matter) applied to them. Holland's severe drinking and driving laws, on the other hand, lump cyclists together with car-drivers rather than pedestrians. A charge of being drunk in charge of a bicycle could result in the loss of your driver's licence.

Bicycles may be built for one, but to the Dutch this seems an unnecessary restriction. Parents fit little seats – one to the crossbar and one to the back carrier – to transport their offspring. Dutch mothers build up sturdy calves pedalling along with one child on the front, one on the back and panniers stuffed with shopping. A burly rugby forward apparently singing in a sweet soprano turns out to be masking a merry mite on the carrier behind him. Courting couples share a bike too, usually with the woman riding side-saddle on the carrier. One of the early lessons of adolescence is learning how far a girl's legs stick out. First dates invariably involve bruised knees.

Neatness

A British magistrate, paying a visit to a Dutch home in the 17th century, was astonished when the housemaid plonked him down on the outside step, plucked off his muddy boots and carried him across the shining hall floor to her mistress's parlour. Around the same period a supperless French cleric complained that the Dutch would sooner die of hunger than disturb the perfect symmetry of the sparkling crockery and glittering cauldrons in their kitchens.

Little has changed. Inside and out Holland appears clipped, scrubbed, washed, polished and freshly painted. Trees in the countryside are planted in lines, and the black-and-white cows are arranged in neat little groups. Battalions of street-sweepers and cleaning machines advance through the cities day and night. Indoors, people scour, buff and tidy to meet the ideal set for them by the poised interiors painted by Old Masters such as Vermeer and Saenredam. Those who fail are accused of having a 'Jan Steen household', after the artist famed for his portrayal of chaotic and debauched tavern scenes.

Just to make sure that householders toe the line, the Environment Police will poke through any garbage bags left outside the demarcated collection points, or deposited in the street on days other than specified collection days. If they come up with anything that has your address on it, you will receive a nasty letter, and possibly a fine.

Culture

Mix and Match

The Dutch are cultural magpies. They keep a beady eye on other people's cultural trends, and are swift to snap up sparkling new fashions. This means that rather than producing an indigenous culture, the Dutch have become voracious consumers of everybody else's – true Europeans, whose cultural fads and fancies know no borders. The Netherlands acts as a giant cultural sponge.

Dutch bookshelves are well-stocked with volumes from Britain, Germany, America and France, often in the original languages. Foreign books are reviewed in the Dutch press long before the translations appear in print. Music from every corner of the globe blasts out of local stereos (the Dutch own more CDs per capita than anyone else). Theatres fill up for German plays and British musicals, and audiences flock to see Spanish and Italian films. Even the Dutch national clichés are not entirely homegrown. Clogs are worn in other muddy northern climes, Delftware is an imitation of Chinese porcelain, and the tulip was brought from Turkey.

Three centuries ago, in the heady years of Holland's Golden Age, Dutch artists (finding no market in a Protestant country for virgins and saints) took to portraying themselves and the people around them. The result was an accurate and intimate portrait of their life and times. Never again has Dutch art succeeded in being quite so Dutch.

The abstract artist Mondriaan – he preferred to drop the second 'a' in his surname to make it sound more French – who was inspired by the Dutch landscape to paint his blocks of vertical and horizontal lines, emigrated to America, and the world claimed his work.

Today Holland hosts more artists per square inch than anywhere else in Europe. Suburban gardens sprout curious bolted sculptures and the interiors of public buildings are adorned with unfathomable paintings. Larger cities have 'Art Libraries' which will loan you original artworks to display at home. These are the products of up-and-coming artists, and have been paid for by the city council, in what amounts to a back-door subsidy of modern art.

True to their mercantile tradition, the Dutch excel at turning around other people's cultural products and adding to their value. The Royal Concertgebouw Orchestra has long ranked with the finest in the world, and is especially famed for its performances of works by Gustav Mahler, an Austrian composer.

The same spirit of adventure and delight in things new that fired the traders of the Dutch East India Company, now fuels theatre companies, dancers and artists – for instance, a modern ballet inspired by the sound of a plug being pulled, and water glugging down the plughole.

The Press

The Dutch are avid readers of newspapers, which most get by subscription rather than from the local newsagent. This means that newspapers are read more at home than on trams or trains. Many command family loyalties that last for generations – especially those like *Trouw* and *Het Parool* that grew up out of the underground press which flourished during the Nazi Occupation.

Apart from *De Telegraaf* (a spicy broadsheet), newspapers tend to be sensible and unsensationalist. The sort of salacious curiosity that fills the British tabloid press is much diluted in Holland, where privacy is respected. Wilder speculation and lurid storylines are the realm of the cheap colour magazines that are standard reading in laundrettes, hairdressers', snack bars and dentists' waiting rooms.

Cafés offer piles of magazines and daily papers, so that if you arrive early you can quickly gen up on an opinion to get you through the rest of the evening. This reading matter also ensures that life can be *gezellig* even if you are alone. Nobody complains if you sit for an entire afternoon over one cup of coffee, devouring every paper and glossy magazine the café has to offer.

Literature

Literature is the one area where Dutch culture has remained an island, made inaccessible by a language incomprehensible to most other Europeans. Paradoxically, it is on this island that the Dutch cultural climate is at its healthiest. Everyone is writing a novel. Producers of television chat shows seem able to tap into an endless supply of writers. Old stalwarts of the genre, such as Frederick Hermans, manage first edition print runs of over 500,000, and even newcomers sell books in the tens of thousands. The English-speaking world is beginning to take note. Writers such as Cees Nooteboom and Harry Mulisch have met with some success in translation, and the vignettes painted by Simon Carmiggelt bring foreign readers as close as they can hope to be to the heart of *gezelligheid*.

The Dutch begin their raids on foreign culture at a young age. Winnie-the-Pooh and the inhabitants of Sesame Street are early victims. They line up alongside locals such as Jip and Janneke – a boy and a girl who live next door to each other and first meet by rubbing noses through the hedge. Jip and Janneke are healthily naughty, but are ever learning about good neighbourliness and correct behaviour. They hold a special place in the nation's heart, and their silhouettes can be found everywhere from lavatory doors to coffee mugs.

Apart from Jip and Janneke, the world of Dutch children's literature is populated by unbearably saintly beings – from the boy who saves the world by keeping his finger in the dyke, to Dik Trom, a fat village lad with a heart of gold who always helps the blind and the poor. Dik may not be much to look at, but, on the inside – as his parents constantly remind everyone – "he's a special boy, and that's a fact". The Dutch grow up believing they are the European Dik Troms.

Custom and Tradition

The Dutch jump at any excuse to hang out the bunting. Important football matches and national holidays are the best reasons of all. Trams have fittings on the front to which the driver can attach flags for special occasions, and most houses are equipped with their own pole-holders. Even a celebratory picnic in the park involves stringing lines of brightly coloured pennants between the trees.

Holland's jolliest national holiday is *Koninginnedag* – the Queen's official birthday, at the end of April. This the Dutch celebrate in good mercantile style by holding an enormous fleamarket. Anyone can sell anything anywhere. National flags, yards of orange cloth (for the House of Orange) and pretty pennants decorate the buildings. Cafés move their business outdoors, *gezelligheid* bursts all bounds and people party in the streets the whole day long. Although millions do this, everything sails smoothly along with impeccable Dutch control and understanding of how to have a good time without upsetting the neighbours.

Not so New Year's Eve, when the point is to terrify as many people as you can with fireworks. Youths lurk in dark doorways to throw crackers at your feet, wags set off whole boxes at once and improvise with tins and bottles to make louder bangs (often maiming themselves in the process). By midnight a cloud of gunpowder smoke hangs over the country and Holland flashes and explodes like a battleground.

Christmas, on the other hand, is a low-key affair. Until recently, few Dutch people bothered much with Christmas. Traditionally, it is *Sinterklaas*, St. Nicholas's day on 6th December, that attracts most festivity. For weeks beforehand, genial, white-haired St. Nicholases traipse through The Netherlands with a servant, Black

Pete, in tow. Black Pete is usually a white person with layers of dark make up, a fuzzy wig and thick red lips. Children are told that he will come in the night and take them away if they are naughty. Curiously, the Dutch see nothing insulting or dangerous in this. The chat show guests who are assembled to discuss the racist implications usually bow to the claims of Tradition. Attempts to undermine the custom – White Pete (a black person with chalky make-up), Green Pete (environmental lobby) and Pink Pete (gay) – usually fall flat.

On the evening of 5th December, Dutch families gather to eat chewy gingerbread and other *Sinterklaas* fare and to swop presents. The gifts are simple, inexpensive and usually make some point about the recipient's character or behaviour. They are accompanied by a poem, penned by the giver, that drives the point home. Less robust nations might think that giving someone a stick of deodorant, with a few neatly rhymed couplets about her bathing habits, is the sort of activity that is bound to end in tears, but to the forthright Dutch it is all a recipe for a jolly good time.

Rites of Passage

One in five Dutch adults lives alone. Vast numbers of others live together as couples, with no social stigma at all. Marriage is respectable, but most Dutch parents would prefer their offspring to live together with some-one for a few years than to marry young. When people do decide to get married they often have two weddings – one in the town hall (to legalise the bond) and one in church (for show). From the legal point of view, a wedding that takes place in church only does not count.

There are also two receptions – a large formal dinner for all the guests, and a subsequent riotous bash for favoured friends. As with many things in Dutch life, propriety and wantonness go hand-in-hand.

Dutch forthrightness dictates that invitations should specify whether or not you are invited to the second party. This gives rise to the most anguished social decision that most Dutch people are ever called on to make. People who thought themselves close friends may be lost for life if they come down on the wrong side of the great divide.

The Dutch say that a wedding starts with glamour, and ends in underwear. This doesn't refer so much to the happy couple, as to the guests at the second party. As the alcohol begins to flow, the sing-along and silly dances begin and the feast becomes Bacchanalian. From time to time a couple of guests disappear for a few minutes and return in costume to act out an (apparently) hilarious sketch. The butt of all these dramatic offerings is the newly wedded couple – their bad habits, repellent quirks and previous amours.

Understandably, funerals are a little more sedate – though generally fairly secular in timbre. Family and friends head off to the *Uitvaartcentrum* (literally: 'departure centre'), where the loved one is despatched to the sound of music (*My Way* and songs by Mieke Telkamp, the Dutch Vera Lynn, currently top the charts). Afterwards everyone gathers in an ante-chamber for coffee and one slice of cake.

The only utterly unforgivable sin in the Dutch canon is to forget somebody's birthday. Every Dutch lavatory has a birthday calendar pinned to the back of the door, so that inhabitants of the house can be sure that they will get a daily reminder of their friends' and relations' big day.

Birthdays are the pivot of a Dutch person's internal

calendar, and the ritual of their celebration is always the same. Close friends and family come for coffee. They will bring flowers, and sometimes a small gift. They will expect to sit in a circle, make polite conversation, sip their coffee and eat their slice of cake. In this they will not be disappointed, though in honour of the occasion a second slice of cake may be offered. There will be colourful paper chains overhead, and flags. A glass of port or sherry will be served to signal the end of the proceedings.

What is Sold Where

Hypermarkets, megamarkets and maximarts are beginning to appear on the outskirts of cities in Holland, but large-scale, impersonal shopping is not really the Dutch way. Small, specialized, neighbourhood stores are more *gezellig*, and the local street-market is probably cheaper. Most people buy supplies daily, rather than in plastiwrapped bulk, and look forward to having a chat and maybe even a cup of coffee while they are about it.

The Dutch cheerily greet the shopkeeper as they come in, and leave with a friendly *"Tot ziens"* ("See you again"). When it is their turn to be served they expect to be allowed all the time in the world to pick and choose and pass the time of day. Tasting your cheese before you buy it, asking the cheeseshop assistant's advice, and deciding whether you want a wedge or a flat cut, is all part of the enjoyment. Outside the shops, brightly painted street organs pipe out tunes that give a festive air to an ordinary activity.

Local trades unions have put a ceiling on weekly opening hours. The Germans, faced with the same problem, shut up shop the moment everybody else is leaving work, close at lunchtime on Saturdays and all day Sunday, and generally turn shopping into a rushed and punishing experience for anyone with a 9 to 5 job. True to the Dutch spirit of compromise – and good business sense – shops in Holland stay open on Saturday afternoons, but close on Monday mornings, when few people could be much bothered to visit them anyway.

After hours, you will find anything from *chorizo* to champagne at the neighbourhood 'night shop', which opens just as other shops close. Fresh flowers – as items essential to Dutch social intercourse – are on sale at all times of night and day from roadside kiosks, night shops and even petrol stations. Coffee, another staple, can be found in the most unexpected places, including the butcher's.

Eating and Drinking

The Feast

Erasmus, the great 16th-century Dutch humanist and man of letters, noted that his countrymen "were not prone to any serious vices except, that is, a little given to pleasure, especially to feasting". Four centuries later the national ability to tuck in and drink up is still impressive. Quantity is as important as quality in Dutch cooking. The national dish, *hutspot* ('hotchpotch'), is a well-boiled stew that was fed to starving citizens after the siege of the city of Leiden, and still requires a similar state of raven-ousness before it can be really enjoyed.

The Dutch breakfast will consist of coffee (in abundance), bread, cheese, flaked chocolate (to scatter on the bread, and thence over the whole table), and just one more cup of coffee. Lunch comprises coffee and a *broodje* – a bread roll with cheese or ham, or served *gezond* ('healthy' – layered with cholesterol-rich cheese, the odd lettuce leaf and an egg thrown in for good measure).

There are one or two coffee breaks in between. Midway through the afternoon you might meet up with a friend for a cup of coffee, in which case you may lash out on a little *gebakje* – usually a slice of apple tart with cream. Curiously, in this land of milk and cheese the only cream that is ever available is thin and watery, or aerated into a tasteless froth. Dinner is early, at around 6 or 7 o'clock, to give you time to pop down to your local café for a beer or a cup of coffee later on.

In between meals the Dutch devour large quantities of potato chips smothered in mayonnaise or, if they are really peckish, served *oorlog* (literally, 'war'), i.e. spattered with ketchup, mayonnaise and one or two other sauces as well. Alternatively, they stop off at a roadside kiosk for a quick raw herring. These are eaten by tossing your head back and slipping a whole fillet down your throat, holding it by the tail. This is an experience that few foreigners undergo.

Killing Vegetables

It seems a particular trait of northern European tribes that the vegetable is seen as an object for all-out assault, using the full battery of implements that the kitchen can provide. The Belgians fry, the Germans pickle, the English boil, and the Dutch mash. Cabbages and potatoes especially, but also endives and peas all end up pounded together in a stolid *stamppot*. Usually greyish-white in hue, with green flecks and the consistency of partially-set concrete, *stamppot* is dished up with another dollop of something meaty.

This fundamental disrespect for the vegetable means that in traditional Dutch cuisine no meal is considered complete without meat. Even pea soup (which should be so thick that you can stand your spoon upright in it) comes with floating sausages and bacon. Fish has honorary status as a vegetable. The 'Vegetarian' section of a menu in a traditional Dutch restaurant will invariably involve cod. In a Dutch household the question "What's for dinner?" gets the answer "Broccoli", or "Spinach", or whatever else the main vegetable is that night. Meat is a given, not a variable.

Not even salads escape the masher. A Dutch salad is 90% potato and mayonnaise, and 10% something else that gives it a name rather than a flavour. Consequently, most salads are creamy white and are only distinguishable from each other by the label. Recent innovations in the field have added virulent yellow (chicken curry salad) and an alarming crimson (American beef salad) to the spectrum.

Foreign Flavours

Recently, Dutch cuisine, like Dutch culture, has recreated itself as a sort of mix-and-match of foreign influences. France was raided first, then the ex-colonies in Indonesia, and lately the Mediterranean and the Orient. The New Dutch kitchen comes up with such delights as saffron tagliatelle with shiitake mushrooms and cream cheese, or pork served with a peanut sauce.

Brave attempts by foreign cuisines to fight back have met with some success. Ethnic restaurants abound, but are suitably tempered to Dutch taste. Curries differ from stew in colour only, and chefs of cuisines noted for the delicacy of their portions, such as the Japanese, have learned to serve larger helpings and add more beef to the menu. *Nouvelle cuisine* was never a great success in Holland. Besides offering mingy portions it gave bad value for money. The most popular foreign meal by far is the Indonesian *rijsttafel*, a personal banquet of rice with a host of side dishes that appeals to the Dutch instinct for feasting.

Drinking

When they are not drinking coffee, the Dutch put away enormous quantities of beer, though they do so genteely, sipping at fluted glasses that hold just a mouthful or two. Serious drinkers hurry things along with a gin chaser, calling the combination a *kopstoot* ('headbanger').

Jenever, the ancestor of British gin, was invented by a Dutch doctor as a diuretic and retains a medicinal tang. It comes in a small glass filled to the brim, so that the first sip has to be taken by lowering your chin to the table. Then you knock back the rest with a single gulp.

If you are lucky, you might get the *Amsterdammetje*: if the last bit of *jenever* in the bottle doesn't quite fill the glass, then you down it for free and get a refill. *Jenever* comes *oud* (old and mellow) or *jong* (young and sharp), and sometimes in lemon or blackberry flavours.

Advocaat is a more idiosyncratic drink, and very much an acquired taste. A sort of alcoholic custard made from raw eggs and cognac, it comes in a glass, but is best tackled with a spoon and makes more sense as a sauce poured over ice-cream.

The favoured place for drinking is a 'brown café' (that

is, one where the walls and ceiling have been stained by decades of tobacco smoke), though on freezing winter's days the Dutch will warm their blood with a quick visit to a *proeflokaal*. These were once free tasting houses attached to a *jenever* merchant's premises. These days you have to pay, but the procedure is much the same: walk in, drink up, walk out.

Health and Hygiene

Endless cups of coffee, frequent nibbles on biscuits and multiple slices of fatty cheese can take their toll on arteries and veins. Yet, although heart disease is Holland's number one killer, the Dutch are a sturdy bunch who manage to live longer, on average, than any other Europeans. They put this down to a natural healthiness that they inherited from their robust farmer ancestors, and continue to tuck in.

Teeth, on the other hand, are a subject of great concern. The condition, maintenance, and cost of repair of teeth rival football and the weather as the most popular topics of Dutch conversation.

Dentists drill and fill, but each practice also has a 'Mouth Hygienist', whose task it is to carry on the time-honoured Dutch activities of scrubbing, scraping, buffing and polishing. Costs pile up, and the health insurance won't always foot the bill. All this trouble and expense does not leave the Dutch with straight, glistening, American-style grins. As in their battle against the ocean, all the hard work simply serves to keep things functional and intact.

Dutch doctors believe in the inherently hardy constitutions of their patients, and for most ailments will advise them to let nature take its course and allow the body to heal itself. Dutch women take a similarly natural approach to childbirth. Nearly half of Dutch babies are born at home, and few Dutch mothers use any sort of anaesthetic or painkiller during birth. Even mothers who have their babies in hospital are packed off home after a day or two. Nature and the World Health Organization approve – Holland is one of the safest places on earth to have a baby.

Hygiene

Though they will spend hours cleaning their houses, the Dutch prefer to get their personal ablutions out of the way as speedily as possible. Showers win out over baths as they are quicker and cheaper to operate. Bathrooms are small. In many you could shower and use the lavatory simultaneously, thus saving even more time. Sometimes there isn't even room for a basin, forcing people to shave and clean their teeth over the kitchen sink. This is not a problem in a Dutch household, as there are never any dirty dishes lying around.

The cleaning of teeth is the only part of the process over which the Dutch may linger, but here time is seen as an investment against outrageous dentists' bills. An armoury of brushes, wooden spikes, mirrors on sticks and metal scrapers all help in the battle against plaque and the ravages of caffeine. These line up alongside the bottles of homeopathic medicines (paid for by health insurance) which help nudge nature along her course when she is proving reluctant. The odd potion or balm inherited (together with all those healthy genes) from rural ancestors also makes an appearance – *uierzalf*, a soothing skin cream made for cows' udders, is a particular favourite.

Systems

Dutch life runs with a quiet efficiency. Trains run on time, streets are cleaned and letters are delivered the day after they are posted, without any fuss, simply as a matter of course. Unlike the Germans, the Dutch are not ostentatious about achieving this order; nor are their systems debilitated by the fetters of tradition, like the English. Good organization helps make life *gezellig*, and is worth whatever it costs – though it doesn't do to flaunt your success at it, and changes that improve old ways are readily accepted.

Respectable citizens participate in life's systems – public and private – with honesty. They are trusted to weigh and label their own fresh produce in supermarkets, without slipping in an extra tomato or handful of mushrooms. They run up tabs at the bar, and don't disappear without paying; they pay their taxes without too much fuss, and frank their own tickets on public transport. People who break this trust can expect to feel the full thrust of social and legal disapprobation. 'Black riders' (or 'grey riders' to the politically correct) who are caught without a valid ticket have to pay an on-the-spot fine that amounts to twenty times the normal fare. If they don't have the money – or some form of identification – on them, doors are sealed and everything comes to a halt while the police are called. Respectable citizens then disapprove even more strongly because they have been made late, and punctuality is fundamental to the smooth running of things.

The Not So Open Road

As Holland is so small and overcrowded, roads have to be squeezed in as best they can. Traffic signs occur every few yards, turning trips across cities into a staccato of stops and starts, and suggesting all sorts of contradictory directions for longer journeys. The Dutch are not confused by this, as once meshed into the knot of motorways they know that they are bound to turn up at their destination sooner or later. If they miss a turning there is sure to be another one further on and, besides, it takes about as much time to cross the entire country as it takes people in London or Berlin to get to work.

Education

Less than a third of Dutch schoolchildren attend conventional state schools. The rest go to schools specific to one of the three *zuilen* – Protestant, Roman Catholic or Montessori/Alternative. Though these establishments are privately run, they get state subsidies, and all children sit the same state exams. The idea of an elite crust of private schools is anathema to the egalitarian Dutch.

Specialization starts early. When they enter secondary school, at around the age of twelve, children are channelled into a course which leads to university, or in the direction of a career qualification.

The Dutch respect a good education and see it as the first step in the process of taking your place in society, shouldering your part of the burden of hard work and earning your just reward. Those that have a university degree do not flaunt it, but feel quite happy at adding the letters to their name on business cards, or being addressed on envelopes as Drs. (short for *Doctorandus*, and not to be confused with the 'Dr.' earned by those who have a doctorate).

The Dutch have reason to consider themselves well-educated: over 20% have been to university or college (compared with 15% of the French population and 4% in Portugal). Get into a conversation about T.S. Eliot, Nietzsche or Proust, and the chances are that a Dutch person will have read the lot in the original language – or will at least be convinced of an innate ability to express an opinion on them.

All males aged over 18 are currently eligible for national military service, if they are not in full-time education – although it ceases to be compulsory in 1996. In the meantime, as Holland does not really need such a big army, in practice most men get out of it by pleading flat feet, insanity, or some other malady. They may also declare themselves conscientious objectors, in which case they do a slightly longer period of community service. When the law changes, lawyers who specialize in getting unwilling national servicemen off the hook are guaranteed to lose a steady income.

Banks

The Dutch prefer their money to be invisible. They frown at extravagance and disapprove of flashing notes around. Bills are paid, personal debts settled and donations made to charity by discreet transfers between bank accounts, rather than by cash or cheque. In some banks, tellers stuff the filthy lucre into a capsule as soon as they get their hands on it, despatching it along a pneumatic tube to unseen inner recesses of the building. Electronic direct debit from shop counters has met with rocketing success, rising from 3 million payments when it was introduced in 1990, to 200 million in 1994.

When they do handle cash, the Dutch like it to have a visual allure. The Netherlands has some of the most beautiful banknotes in the world, imaginatively covered with birds, sunflowers and a spectrum of pretty colours, and thoughtfully provided with raised bumps so that blind people can read the denominations. It would never do to spend more than you have to, especially by mistake.

Crime and Punishment

The Dutch combine two qualities which most other nations find mutually exclusive – regulated efficiency and laissez faire. The Italians blatantly break rules, the Germans apply them obsessively in the quest for *Ordnung*. The English bicker for ages over the niceties of regulations, then heed them to the letter. The Dutch will enforce a law when it seems sensible to do so, and ignore it when it does not. All officials have one blind eye and a permanent crick in the neck.

Contrary to popular belief, selling marijuana is not legal in Holland. This, and many such activities, are *gedoogd* – not legal but nevertheless 'allowed' in certain controlled areas, to reduce the crime and nastiness that often surround them. The Dutch believe that by letting a little evil in, they can keep the big evil out. In the same way as they will open the locks to allow in a controlled measure of water – taking the pressure off the dykes and thus averting havoc – they will permit a manageable degree of sin in order to prevent being inundated by wholesale debauchery.

Most Dutch people will agree that it is simply common sense to allow prostitutes to work openly, protected from pimps and with access to free medical check-ups. In Holland, prostitutes find themselves at loggerheads not with the moralists or the Law, but with feminists, who feel that they are letting the side down.

When the Dutch tax office decided it was time to crack down on illegal workers in bars and cafés, the inspectors, in the spirit of fair play, published the dates of their 'raids' well in advance. This allowed small-time moonlighters to lie low, and meant that only establishments that had been cooking the books in a big way, and who couldn't possibly disguise the fact, got caught.

The Police

The Dutch police come in all colours and genders, and can be found in pairs, clad in trendy bomber jackets and well-cut trousers, often on mountain bikes, sometimes on horses, but generally as a background presence.

Everybody is so busy being neighbourly, tolerant, *gezellig* and generally well-behaved that the police are left at a bit of a loose end. In some cities, to add to their troubles, they may find that the *Stadswacht* takes work off their hands.

Unarmed, and less fashionably dressed than the police, the *Stadswacht* make sure that everyone continues to be neighbourly, tolerant, *gezellig* and well-behaved. A modern-day version of the old City Watch, the *Stadswacht* is made up largely of long-term unemployed people to whom the authorities have given a uniform, a salary and responsibility – thus, with typical Dutch ingenuity, killing two birds with one stone. The police are left free to pursue hard drugs-dealers and other vicious criminals.

The liberal Dutch attitude towards cannabis does not extend to hard drugs, but it does attract 'drug tourists' to The Netherlands. Although the Dutch have the lowest number of hard-drug addicts per capita in Europe, large cities are nevertheless left with a drugs problem, which manifests itself mainly in petty theft. True to the Dutch spirit of seeing both sides of a problem, the police initiated legislation making it illegal to leave your car unlocked, or unattended with the keys in the ignition.

Bicycle theft is a national pastime. The Dutch spend more on hefty, supposedly foolproof locks than they do on the cycle itself. When a bicycle is stolen it is the loss of the lock that is most lamented. A replacement bicycle is easily come by – simply walk up to a group of cyclists and say loudly and authoritatively "That's *my* bike!". Someone is sure to get off and run away.

Prisons

Convicts languishing in Greek gaols, or stuffed into cells in Britain, dream of Dutch prisons. Yet, not satisfied with cable television, conjugal visiting rights and other comforts, Dutch prisoners have been known to complain about the unfriendliness of the guards, or that the food is fattening.

Dutch prisons are so popular that they have waiting lists of applicants for cells. Unless someone has committed a particularly heinous crime, they will be sentenced to community service, or be issued with a slip of paper which, rather like the tickets in the post office queue, puts them in line for the next cell available.

Government and Bureaucracy

Unlike the British (whose leaders form a distant, detested and self-interested class), the Dutch tend to respect their politicians, and to trust them. Dutch television interviewers are respectful lambs by comparison with the anarchic BBC tigers. Cabinet ministers and city burgomasters wield tremendous executive power, but the Dutch see them as 'one of us', important cogs in an egalitarian machine.

Surprisingly, in Holland, where democracy and egalitarianism are so important, the Queen has a hands-on role in government. (The sovereign is not just a figurehead to be dressed up and wheeled out to snip at ribbons and break champagne bottles over the bows of ships; she turns up for work daily and enjoys a widespread respect.)

Cabinet Ministers are appointed by the Queen and have the right to speak, but not vote, in the Dutch Parliament (which is called the States-General and consists of an elected Lower and Upper House). Legislation starts at the top with the relevant Cabinet Minister and passes downwards for approval by Parliament more often than the other way around.

In cities power is also centralised with mayors, who are appointed rather than elected, holding extraordinary sway.

Politics

There is a saying that if you put two Dutch people in a room they will start a debate; add a third and they will found a church or a political party. Dutch Tolerance and the belief in giving everybody a hearing gives Holland an abundance of political parties. Proportional representation at elections means that many of them win seats in parliament. Yet the States-General is not a bicker box. Members of Parliament spend their time not at each other's throats, but in the time-honoured occupations of negotiation, compromise and working out coalition governments.

Bureaucracy

For the person-in-the-street, tolerance and negotiation come to a juddering halt against a single phrase: *"Dat kan niet"* ("That is not possible"). Dutch people know that when they hear these words, it is time to give up and go home. *Dat kan niet* is the ultimate weapon of minor officials and dedicated bureaucrats.

Like armies, bureaucracies the world over attract similar personalities. Dutch people who feel ill at ease with the national inclination towards flexibility dream of a job in the corridors of petty power. And once they have set their heart on something, they do it well. They learn *Catch 22* off pat, take out the red tape and prepare to tie you in knots. If you catch them off guard, spot a loophole, or try to introduce an element of rationality into your relationship, they counter with *Dat kan niet* – and that's final.

Business

The Dutch invented the multinational. The VOC (Dutch East India Company) was, for two centuries, the largest and most powerful trade organization in the world. Today Philips, Unilever and Royal Dutch Shell (together with two other companies that are not household names) employ a quarter of the Netherlands' workforce. The Dutch don't stop here, but export managers to take control of foreign multinationals. Their linguistic and negotiating prowess, as well as an ability to keep a tight control on the purse strings, quickly propel them to the top of the board.

Dutch merchant ships have given way to pantechnicons – 40% of all international trucking in Europe is Dutch operated. True to the spirit of their trading forefathers, the Dutch remain adept middlemen, deftly turning around other people's products to make a profit. They import chemicals to make fertilizer, then use gas (their sole natural resource) to heat vast greenhouses that supply the markets of Europe with tomatoes, cucumbers, tulips, carnations, fresias, and much more. Over 60% of the world's cut flowers and 50% of its pot plants pass through Holland's gigantic auction houses, though not all of them are homegrown. The Dutch have such a hold on the market that, in order to realise the best prices, farmers in other countries send their blooms to Holland to be sold – for the florist up the road to re-import them.

Dutch openness extends to the Dutch economy. Making too much fuss about regulations and restrictions is bad for trade, and the financial market is no exception to the rule. Centuries ago, the Amsterdam Bank of Exchange was the biggest commercial bank in the world. Foreign monarchs used it for loans to finance their military campaigns, and also to stash away nest eggs in case they were toppled from power. Today, the Dutch guilder is officially linked to the Deutschmark, hitching a ride that makes it one of the strongest currencies in Europe and once again attracts droves of foreign investors.

Dutch frugality appears in business as well as in private life. A visiting businessperson, used to expense account lunches, will be sorely disappointed in The Netherlands. Anything more than coffee and a cheese *broodje* is frowned upon as needlessly extravagant and a waste of time. Business hours are for business. Similarly, offices are modest to the point of austerity, and even letterheads and logos are suitably subdued.

Bosses and Workers

The key word in a Dutch company is teamwork. (Like most other key words in the Dutch business vocabulary, it is said in English). Dutch business, like Dutch country-side, is organized horizontally rather than vertically. Co-operation, negotiation and consensus opinion are the mainspring of Dutch business. Endless meetings are their result.

Like cafés, meetings provide ample ground for the exercising of opinions. The difference is that in a meeting the speakers must back their opinions with careful and comprehensive research. This gives them the confidence to express the opinions with an energy and resolution that other nations might find intimidating. But, in the end, there is a lot of give and take. The aim of a meeting is not to outvote a minority, but to reach a joint decision that the team can happily implement. Foreigners less used to such forthright cut and thrust, however, may be left bleeding by the wayside.

Rigid hierarchies are contrary to team spirit, and don't fit in with the Dutch view of an egalitarian society. Everyone from the office cleaner to the managing director is a company *medewerker* – a 'co-worker'. In a Dutch company 'supervisors' are 'co-ordinators', and though the boss might be addressed as *U*, he – or she – knows better than to even think of issuing anything that might be taken to resemble an order. (In The Netherlands big bosses are far more likely to be 'he'. Although women are readily accepted as equal members of the team, and even as co-ordinators, there are just a handful of women in senior management.)

One-upmanship and flaunting your individual abilities will alienate members of the team, and are not the way to go about getting promotion. That comes through hard work, a good co-operative spirit and the right education. Decisions made at the beginning of secondary school about which educational channel to follow, set Dutch workers on a course for life. Few people make it from the factory floor to the accounts department, let alone the boardroom.

On the other hand, Dutch people cite 'ambition' as the second most important criterion (after hard work and ahead of education) for getting on in life. Overt parading of your superiority might be unacceptable, but behind-the-scenes schemes and stratagems are just as complex and as effective in Dutch companies as in any others. Subtle signs stake out one's progress: the Dutch dress informally at work. Jeans and open-necked shirts are quite acceptable male attire. Dark suits are the preserve of very top management. Jeans combined with a jacket and tie mark the first step towards higher things. Next, jeans are dropped in favour of proper trousers. This sartorial signalling is subtly controlled. Dressing above one's station is contrary to good team spirit.

Even though the separation of workers and management is the closest that Dutch society comes to a class system, industrial relations are good. Negotiations between trades unions and management are non-confrontational. The law (and not only the ethos of teamwork) dictates that companies employing more than 35 people should set up an *ondernemingsrad* – a workers' council that has to be consulted on all major policy changes and on any matter relating to personnel. Even in smaller organizations, the workers are entitled to hold meetings twice a year in order to question the board about the running of the company. Outside of office hours these divisions dissolve, and *medewerkers* are quite happy to wander down to the café and become *mede-* drinkers.

Language

Adept traders though they be, the Dutch have found it hard to export their language. Its guttural 'g' has potential clients muttering about diseases of the throat, and foreign lips and tongues give out entirely when trying to wrap themselves around 'ui'. The English dismiss anything they find too baffling as 'Double Dutch'. Van Gogh knew all too well the problems that his mother tongue gave others, so he signed his paintings 'Vincent' in the hope that gallerists would find that easier to pronounce than his surname.

The Dutch have, on the other hand, never been shy about importing words from other languages. In Holland everyone stops work for the 'weekend', says 'sorry' if they bump into you and enjoys freshly squeezed *jus d'orange*. They are famously proficient at speaking languages other than their own, and even manage to make some improvements with their mistakes – such as when they talk of a 'crowdy' room, or the laborious task of 'ironating' clothes.

Occasionally the Dutch have found the inaccessibility of their language a convenient screen. When Napoleon invaded The Netherlands he forced the Dutch to adopt surnames – something they had not thought of doing before then. Assuming that this would be a temporary measure, and that once the invader had been sent packing they could resort to their old way of life, people thought up all sorts of odd names so that they could have a good laugh at the unwitting French officials' expense. But the joke backfired. Today there are families burdened with such names as *Naaktgeboren* ('born naked'), *Hoogenboezem* ('high bosomed'), *Poepjens* ('pooh-pooh'), or the tongue-twisting (even for the Dutch) *Gigengak*.

You can hear variations of Dutch spoken in Belgium (Flemish, or *Vlaams*) and among the descendants of the Boers in South Africa (*Afrikaans*). Though they will tell you derisory jokes about the Belgians, the Dutch rather envy the soft, melodic tones of *Vlaams*. *Afrikaans*, on the other hand, will send the average Dutch person into fits of giggles, sounding to their ears like archaic baby talk.

Historically, Dutch is related to German, though it lacks the Teutonic gloss and edge. It is a softer, comfier, muddier tongue that seems to have grown up out of the bogs and polders – a *gezellige* language. The Dutch take the hard edge off any number of words by adding the diminutive *tje* or *je*. Thus, in their cosy neighbourhood café they will order a *pilsje* in preference to a pils, and cash dispensing machines will invite you to insert your *pasje*. Friends and family get the same treatment. There can be nothing more *gezellig* than sitting down to a *kopje koffie* with Aunty Truusje.

The Author

Rodney Bolt was born in Africa, has an Irish passport, a British driving licence and a Dutch residence permit. Having lived and worked in Greece, in England and in Germany, he has finally come to roost in Amsterdam, where such hybrid creatures pass unnoticed, and are even made to feel at home.

For many years he ran a pub theatre in London, and has worked as a theatre director, English teacher, private tutor, letter-sorter and journalist. Now he makes his living mainly from travel writing, and is failing to fend off the Dutch desire to write novels.

He divides his national affections between The Netherlands and Madeira, just as he hopes one day to divide his domestic arrangements between a canal house and a *quinta* in the hills. In the meantime he lives in one corner of a large 19th-century house, within walking distance of a street-market, a swimming pool and three excellent museums. He could ask for little more.